Basher™

# STEM Junior

# SCIENCE

KINGFISHER

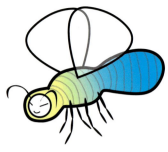

# KINGFISHER

First published in 2020 by Kingfisher
an imprint of Macmillan Children's Books
6 Briset Street, London EC1M 5NR
Associated companies throughout the world
www.panmacmillan.com

Text and design copyright © Toucan Books Ltd 2020
Illustrations copyright © Simon Basher 2020
www.basherscience.com

Author: Jonathan O'Callaghan
Consultants: Robin Ulster and James Denby
Editor: Anna Southgate
Designer: Leah Germann
Proofreader: Rachel Malig
Indexer: Marie Lorimer

Dedicated to Baxter Lawrence

ISBN 978-0-7534-4512-9

A CIP catalogue record for this book is available
from the British Library

Printed in China

9 8 7 6 5 4 3 2 1
1TR/0420/WKT/UG/128MA

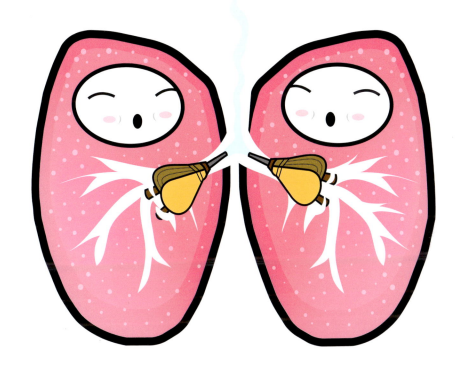

# Contents

# Go Science!

All aboard for the most fantastic science tour EVER. Hosted by a bunch of chatty types who specialize in biology, physics and chemistry, this is one wild ride. First up, meet the Lively Critters – from Bacteria to Mammal, these are the weird and wonderful creatures that inhabit planet Earth. Then come the Body Bits, those vital systems that keep your heart ticking and your blood racing. Join the Physics Crew to find out what makes up the universe – everything around you depends on this motley bunch! Last but not least come the Lab Rats. By the time these chemistry specialists are done you'll know Gas from Solid and Melting Point from Boiling Point. Hey, get your lab coat on, there's not a moment to lose.

**Bacteria and Virus**

**Plant**

**Invertebrate**

**Arthropod**

**Insect**

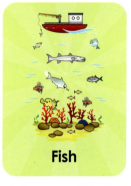

**Fish**

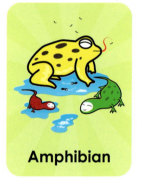

**Amphibian**

**Reptile**

**Bird**

**Mammal**

# Lively Critters

Are you ready to meet the incredible life forms that inhabit planet Earth? From Bacteria to Mammal, you won't believe how many different types of living things there are. Each one of these Lively Critters is just itching to swim, crawl, fly and walk you through its world.

You'll meet characters with backbone (and without) and learn about the different places they inhabit – land, air and sea. Along the way, you'll learn how these critters move, breathe and multiply to keep Earth teeming with thousands of weird and wonderful creatures.

# Bacteria and Virus

⭐ Minuscule Marvels

## THE BIG IDEA

Tiny types of life and **cells** that inhabit the world around us. They are everywhere, but are too small to see with the naked eye.

Did you know that living things can be really tiny? It's true, and some of the smallest critters are forms of me, Bacteria! Look at me under a microscope and you'll see just one single cell. Pretty basic, huh? I reproduce by making copies of myself. You have bacteria inside you. Some are good for you, while others can cause infections and disease.

My buddy Virus is an infectious type too, but even smaller than me (and, I think, nastier). This tiny group of **molecules** isn't really alive at all, but needs to be inside something else that's living in order to survive. That could be you. . .

- ◉ All life on Earth probably began with bacteria 3.5 billion years ago

- ◉ Scientists think there are five million trillion trillion bacteria on Earth

## SAY WHAT?

**Cell:** The smallest basic unit of a plant or animal. All living things are made up of cells.

**Molecule:** A group of atoms (see page 48) joined together.

## SCIENCE NOW

Life on Earth exists in biomes – places that have the right soil, temperature and other conditions to suit certain kinds of life. Viruses and bacteria need biomes, too. One biome they particularly enjoy is inside your intestines.

# Plant

## ★ Green Go-Getter

**THE BIG IDEA**

An **organism** made of lots of rigid cells. It turns sunlight into energy and often relies on animals or the wind to spread its seeds.

Hi, I'm Plant, a living organism that usually (but not always) has a stem, leaves and flowers. I can be a tree, a shrub, a herb, grass and even moss. I often change my appearance with the seasons.

I like to stay in one spot, with my roots heading underground to collect water. I'm so smart, I make my own food by turning sunlight into energy, a process called photosynthesis. I do this using chlorophyll – a green substance in my cells. Sometimes I bear fruits and flowers with seeds inside them. They grow to make new plants if the conditions are right.

- There are about 400,000 species of plant in the world

- The largest flowering plant is found in Indonesia. Called *Rafflesia arnoldii*, its flower measures 1 m (3 ft) across!

## SAY WHAT?

**Organism:** Any type of life, such as a plant or animal. It can be made of a single cell, or lots of different types of cells.

## ☀ SCIENCE NOW

Research has suggested that plants actually have a type of intelligence. They can learn things and react to their world. They can even solve problems, such as finding food and water. Not everyone agrees with this idea, however!

# Invertebrate
## ★ Super Softy

### THE BIG IDEA

An animal without a **backbone**. Groups of invertebrates include sponges, **molluscs** and arthropods such as insects and spiders.

Don't you start! Yes, I'm Invertebrate and, yes, I have no backbone, but you can't accuse me of being spineless. I make up more than 90% of all Earth's creatures so there must be something gutsy about me, wouldn't you say?

I can be anything from a worm or slug (ew!) to a spider or jellyfish, and any insect you care to think of. I live on land and in water and come in a multitude of shapes and sizes from diddy flea to giant squid. Some of my forms have hard outer shells to protect their soft and squidgy bodies – Arthropod will tell you more.

- ◉ The longest invertebrate is the ribbon worm. It can reach 55 m (180 ft) long

- ◉ Some types of invertebrate, such as starfish, have no heads!

### SAY WHAT?

**Backbone:** A set of connected bones that run down the middle of an animal's back.

**Mollusc:** Invertebrate with a soft, unsegmented body and often a shell (e.g. clam, mussel, snail).

### ✱ SCIENCE NOW ✱

The world's largest invertebrate is the colossal squid. It can measure up to 14 m (46 ft), which is longer than a bus, and can weigh a massive 750 kg (1650 lb) – about the same as 12 people.

# Arthropod

## ★ Bit Player

**THE BIG IDEA**

An invertebrate with a solid exoskeleton. An arthropod's body is usually separated into different pieces known as **segments**.

A creature of several parts, I'm Arthropod – an invertebrate with a solid outer shell. Crustaceans such as crabs and lobsters are arthropods. So are insects and spiders.

My shell is called an external skeleton or exoskeleton. Beneath it I'm symmetrical, which means both sides of my body are the same. I'm also arranged in segments that join together to make a larger body! If you looked at a centipede, you'd see that each pair of legs is attached to one segment. And when I need to grow, I simply shed my exoskeleton and form a larger one in its place.

- ◉ Arthropods existed 500–600 million years ago – and were the first animals to walk on the ground

- ◉ The world's largest land-living arthropod is the coconut crab; it can weigh up to 4 kg (9 lb) and has a 20-cm-wide (8 in) shell

**SAY WHAT?**

**Segment:** One part of a whole thing. Something can be separated into segments, and each of them adds together to make the whole.

**SCIENCE NOW**

An arthropod's body layout is different to that of a human and its brain surrounds its food pipe. This means that, whenever an arthropod eats, the food passes through its brain.

# Insect
## ★ Creepy Crawly

**THE BIG IDEA**

The most common type of arthropod, an insect has three segments and six legs.

Look at me, creepy crawly Insect! You know Arthropod, with its tougher outer skeleton? Well, I'm one! An insect is an arthropod with three segments and six legs.

Head, thorax, abdomen – those are my segments. My head is where my brain is located, along with my eyes and antennae to feel and smell things. My thorax comes next, with legs and wings attached (if I can fly). Then comes my abdomen, complete with the **organs** I need to digest food and reproduce. Don't confuse me with an arachnid (that's a spider to you). Those arthropods have two segments and eight legs!

- ◉ Some insects can walk on the surface of water

- ◉ A ladybird will eat more than 5000 smaller insects in its lifetime

- ◉ The first living things sent to space were insects – fruit flies!

### SAY WHAT?

**Organ:** A group of **tissues** that perform a certain function inside a living thing; the heart or lungs, for example.

**Tissue:** Another word for various materials that make up a living body.

### ✳ SCIENCE NOW ✳

Insect eyes are not like human eyes. Called compound eyes, they are made up of lots of smaller eyes joined together. It means that insects can see a much wider area than humans can. Sometimes they have extra eyes, called ocelli, on top of their heads.

# Fish

## ★ Super Swimmer

### THE BIG IDEA

A vertebrate animal that uses fins to swim in water. It breathes by taking **oxygen** from the water using its gills.

I'm Fish, a slippery type that lives in water. You'll find me swimming in oceans, rivers and lakes. There are many different types of fish in the world and some (but not all) are covered in tiny plates called scales.

Shaped like a torpedo, I have fins to propel me through water – sometimes at great speed – and for steering when I want to change direction. I breathe using fleshy gills, which absorb oxygen from water passing over their surfaces. I'm a vertebrate, which means I have a backbone. Some fish have hard skeletons while others, such as sharks (yes, a shark is a fish), have softer skeletons made of **cartilage**.

- ◉ The biggest fish in the world is the whale shark, which can measure up to 21 m (70 ft) long

- ◉ More than 30,000 species of fish have been found in the world so far

### SAY WHAT?

**Oxygen:** The third most common element in the universe. Life depends on oxygen to survive.

**Cartilage:** A type of tissue that has a similar function to bone, but is softer and more flexible.

### ✳ FABULOUS FIND ✳

Some fish live really deep down in the ocean. The deepest found so far is *Pseudoliparis swirei*, a type of snailfish 7966 m (26,135 ft) underwater in the Mariana Trench in the Pacific Ocean. Scientists think this might be the greatest depth a fish can survive.

# Amphibian

## ★ Multi-Tasker

**THE BIG IDEA**

An animal that lives both in water and on land. Amphibians are cold-blooded vertebrates that lay eggs.

Yes, I'm slimy, a bit gross even, but I'm also very cool – literally. I'm Amphibian, a cold-blooded vertebrate, whose body temperature adapts to my surroundings. Mostly four-legged, my kind include salamanders, frogs, newts and toads.

I can live both in the water and on land, using gills and lungs to breathe. I have quite wet skin and a wide mouth for catching prey. To reproduce, I lay eggs in water. My young forms look different to my adult forms, thanks to a process called **metamorphosis**. But you know this surely – it's how a tadpole turns into a frog.

**SAY WHAT?**

**Metamorphosis:** A process by which some animals change from a younger form to their adult self – for example, when a caterpillar turns into a butterfly.

- Many amphibians have thin skin to help absorb water from the air when on dry land, so keeping them moist

- The giant palm salamander's tongue is the most powerful muscle in the animal kingdom! It can move 50 times faster than you can blink

**SCIENCE NOW**

Many amphibians eat their food whole and swallow it without even chewing! They eat live critters, sometimes using their tongues to grab them and pull them into their mouths. Tasty!

# Reptile
⭐ Dry Dweller

## THE BIG IDEA

An animal with dry skin that mostly lives on land. Reptiles are cold-blooded vertebrates that lay eggs.

You've met cold-blooded Amphibian? Well I'm cold-blooded and a vertebrate too, but I have dry skin. I'm Reptile – I live both on land and in water, and sometimes even in scorching hot deserts.

Sometimes my skin is covered in scales or plates – think snake, lizard, tortoise, crocodile. I lay eggs and usually have four legs for running super fast to catch my prey! Of course, snakes have no legs, but use their slithery bodies to slide along the ground! My body is normally quite long and I sometimes have a tail, which I can use as a weapon when defending myself.

- ◉ The fastest reptile in the world is the bearded dragon, which can reach speeds of 40 kmh (25 mph)

- ◉ The longest snake, the reticulated python, typically grows to 6.5 m (21 ft)

### SCIENCE NOW

Crocodiles existed with the dinosaurs, the earliest **species** stretching back 200 million years in time. There are now 23 different species of crocodile found in 90 countries around the world.

# Bird

## ⭐ High Flyer

**THE BIG IDEA**

A vertebrate animal with two legs, wings and feathers. Birds lay eggs and many make nests for their young. Not all birds can fly.

Tweet tweet! You'll see me flying around, but what am I? I'm Bird! A vertebrate, I flap my wings to fly through the sky, using my tail to help me steer. I usually have two legs and feathers, which are sometimes colourful to attract a mate. I have a beak or a bill to catch prey and eat.

As with Amphibian and Reptile, my young hatch from eggs. But unlike them I'm warm-blooded, which means I can create my own heat. But what about my feet? Look closely and you'll see they're not all that different from dinosaur feet. In fact, most scientists think dinosaurs (now **extinct**) might be my distant relatives!

- The largest bird in the world is the ostrich, reaching 2.8 m (9.2 ft) tall

- The bones of many birds are hollow, which makes them light for flying

**SAY WHAT?**

**Extinct:** A species that has died out completely, and has no living members left on Earth.

**SCIENCE NOW**

Some birds aren't able to flap their wings strongly enough to take off. They are known as flightless birds. Penguins are one example of this, as are chickens, which can't fly far. The dodo is a very famous bird that wasn't able to fly. No surprises that it's now extinct!

# Mammal

## ★ Smart Set

**THE BIG IDEA**

A warm-blooded vertebrate animal that gives birth to its babies, rather than laying eggs. Mammals feed their young on milk.

Hey pal, I'm Mammal . . . and so are you! Yep, humans belong to a group of warm-blooded creatures that live the world over. We have some things in common, but are a mixed bunch, too. Let me tell you more.

Some of us, such as whales, swim in oceans, while others, such as monkeys, live in trees. Others like to live on the ground (that's you). Most of us have hair, or fur even, and our jaws are connected to our skulls. We use ears to listen to sounds, and **lungs** to breathe oxygen. Best of all, we have large brains that make us super clever. It means we can solve problems more easily than other animals.

- All land mammals have four limbs; in the case of humans, that's two arms and two legs

- There's only one mammal that can fly: a bat

### SAY WHAT?

**Lung:** An organ that expands and contracts to draw air into the body. The lungs extract oxygen from the air and pass it into the circulatory system (see Chapter 2).

### SCIENCE NOW

Unlike amphibians and reptiles, mammals give birth to live young. Babies develop inside a mother's womb. After birth, they often rely on the mother's milk in order to survive. They then continue to grow until they reach adulthood.

**Skeletal System**

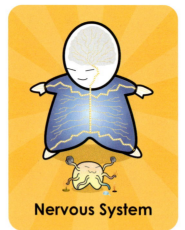

**Nervous System**

**Muscular System**

**Respiratory System**

**Circulatory System**

**Digestive System**

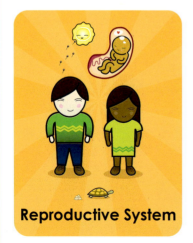

**Reproductive System**

**Urinary System**

# Body Bits

Do you know how many bones your body has in it?
Or how you're able to breathe, move your hands and
even process food? If not, you're in luck, because this
team of Body Bits experts is about to spill the beans!

The human body is a true marvel of nature with many
fascinating things going on inside it. But what makes
it all tick? Come and meet the main systems at work
inside your body and find out what role each of them
has to play. From Skeletal System right through
to Urinary System, you simply couldn't live
without these Body Bits buddies.

# Skeletal System

## ★ Bone Boss

**THE BIG IDEA**

The arrangement of bones holding the human body together.

Take a look inside your body with me, Skeletal System! I make up your skeleton – that's all the different bones holding you together – and you have plenty of them! Each bone is made mostly of tough calcium phosphate on the outside and has spongy **marrow** on the inside.

Starting at your feet, I run up your back and all the way to the skull inside your head. Having a backbone makes you a vertebrate, along with fewer than 10% of all animals. It's me that gives your body shape. I support and protect the different organs in your body and team up with Muscular System to help you move about.

- ◉ The smallest bone is in the ear; it's called the stapes or stirrup

- ◉ Hands and feet contain more than half a human being's bones!

- ◉ An adult human has 206 bones

**SAY WHAT?**

**Marrow:** The soft, sponge-like tissue in the centre of most bones. It's the place where new blood cells are made.

**SMART SCIENTIST**

In the 2nd century, the Greek physician Galen of Pergamon noted how our bones help protect our bodies. He was even able to work out their shapes and how much they weigh. His work remained accepted in Europe for 1500 years.

# Nervous System

## ⭐ Brain Power

### THE BIG IDEA

A network of **nerves** inside the human body. It carries signals to and from the brain, so that the body can perform actions.

How does your brain tell the rest of your body what to do? Why, using me, of course, Nervous System. I'm a network of nerves all over your body, delivering messages at lightning speeds.

Move your hand or blink an eye – those actions happen because your brain sends a signal along my network. Sometimes you control these actions yourself – when picking something up, for example. But what if you touch a really hot surface? My super-sensitive nerve endings send pain signals to your brain (ouch), and then your spinal cord tells your hand to move away. That's an involuntary action.

- ◉ Actions you control are called voluntary actions

- ◉ Actions you can't control are called involuntary actions

### ⚡ SAY WHAT? ⚡

**Nerve:** A bundle of fibres (a bit like wires) made of long chains of nerve cells. They carry signals around the body.

### ✳ REAL WORLD VIEW ✳

There is a machine that can watch as the brain fires out its commands. It's called an MRI (magnetic resonance imaging) scanner. It can produce an image of the brain, so that doctors can watch it in action.

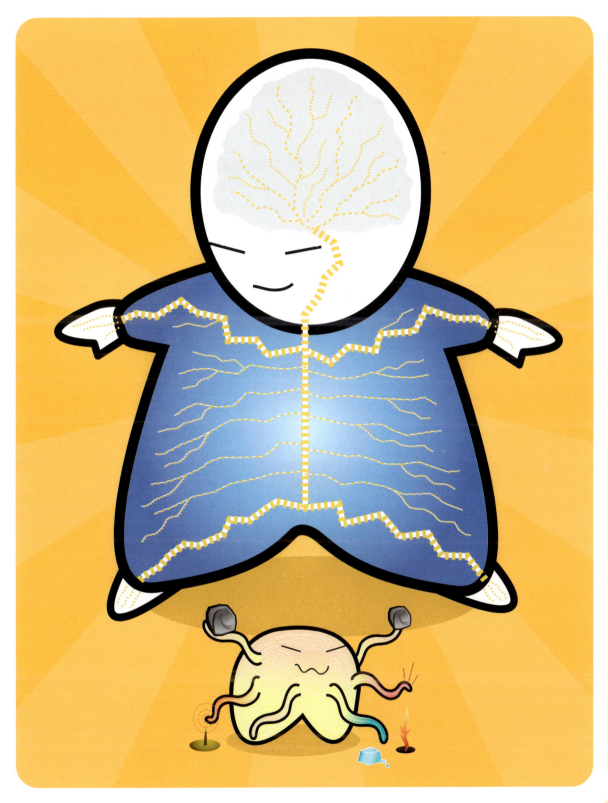

# Muscular System
## ⭐ Mega Mover

**THE BIG IDEA**

The collection of **muscles** in the human body. Many sit beneath the skin, covering the bones, and work to help the body move.

Want to budge from one spot to another? Fancy lifting a juicy apple to your mouth? Well you're going to need some muscle, and that's where I come in. I'm Muscular System. Your body uses me to perform each and every action – walking, talking, lifting, shifting – you name it.

I feature three types of muscle: skeletal, smooth and cardiac. Taking orders from Nervous System, I use the first type to work with Skeletal System, pushing and pulling body parts around. You'll find the second type inside organs such as your stomach, but you don't control these. And cardiac? Well, that's your heart. Thump! Thump!

- ◉ There are more than 600 muscles in the human body

- ◉ When a muscle runs out of energy, the body needs to give it more oxygen to make it work; that's why you feel out of breath

**⚡ SAY WHAT? ⚡**

**Muscle:** A bundle of tissue and fibres that can contract or relax on receiving a signal via the nervous system.

**✳ SCIENCE NOW ✳**

The muscles in your body have different shapes and sizes. For example, the deltoid muscles in your shoulders are triangular, while the muscles in your shoulder blades are saw-shaped. And your bottom has three muscles: one big, one medium-sized and one small!

# Respiratory System

## ★ Big Breather

**THE BIG IDEA**

The system of drawing air into and out of the body to provide oxygen for cells and to remove **carbon dioxide**.

Breathe in . . . and breathe out. You've just seen me in action. My name is Respiratory System – I provide all the oxygen your body needs to stay alive.

When you breathe in, air enters your body through your nose and mouth and travels down your windpipe into your lungs. Your lungs control the flow of air into and out of your body. They take oxygen from the air, and pass it into the bloodstream for transportation around the body. As blood returns to the lungs, it drops off carbon dioxide. Your lungs simply push this waste gas out of your body when you breathe out. In . . . out, in . . . out, in . . .

- ◉ In humans, the left lung is smaller than your right one, to allow room for the heart

- ◉ The lungs, when full of air, are the only organs that would float on water

**SAY WHAT?**

**Carbon dioxide:** The colourless, sour-tasting gas that is a waste product of respiration.

**✳ SMART SCIENTIST ✳**

During the 13th century, Arabian physician Ibn Al-Nafis was the first person to realize that blood travels through the lungs, into the heart, and is then pumped back out into the body.

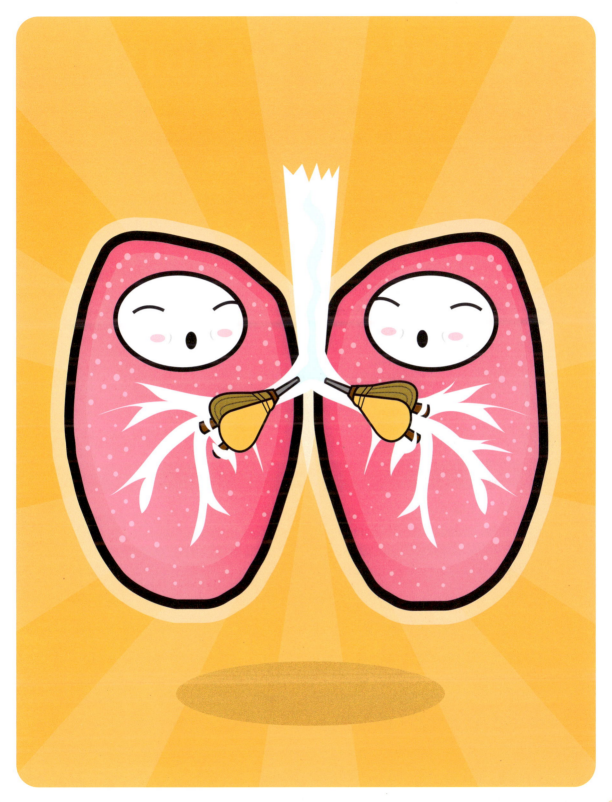

# Circulatory System

⭐ Power Pumper

**THE BIG IDEA**

A system of organs and tubes that transports everything your cells and organs need to operate, and gets rid of their waste.

Hi, I'm Circulatory System and I transport blood around your body! My tireless pulsing network has three main parts.

First comes blood, a red fluid loaded with oxygen, water and **nutrients** – all essential for your cells. Then there is a network of tiny tubes called vessels. Blood has to travel through this network in order to get from one body part to the next. Not only does it carry life-giving substances to your cells, it also takes away waste products such as carbon dioxide. Finally comes the heart. This muscular organ does the hardest work, pumping away day in, day out to keep blood on the move.

◉ Your body contains about 5 litres (9 pints) of blood

◉ Your heart beats about 100,000 times each day, and around 35 million times every year. Over an average lifetime, it beats more than 2.5 billion times!

 **SAY WHAT?**

**Nutrient:** The name given to any substance that helps an organism grow. Humans get their nutrients from the food that they eat.

**✳ REAL WORLD ✳**

When it comes to circulation, the bigger an animal is, the slower its heart pumps blood. On average, the human heart beats 60–100 times a minute. The heart of a blue whale beats just five times a minute, while a shrew's heart beats more than 1000 times!

# Digestive System
## ★ Food Fiend

### THE BIG IDEA

The system that breaks food down to provide the human body with energy.

Chomp, chomp! I'm Digestive System, your in-built food processor. I extract all the nutrients you need to be healthy, while stripping out the waste.

My routine starts in your mouth. As you chew, my saliva begins to break down the food. When you swallow, the food passes down your **oesophagus** into your stomach, where it mixes with bile from your liver. This fluid breaks the food down even more, sped up by substances called enzymes. Your body takes anything useful from what is now mush, and the stuff you don't need passes through your intestines and exits your body when you use the toilet.

- The average human digestive system is 9 m (30 ft) long

- Teeth grind away at food to cut it up into smaller pieces

- Saliva makes the food slippery and easier to swallow

### SAY WHAT?

**Oesophagus:** A tube that connects your throat to your stomach.

### ☀ SMART SCIENTIST

German physician Rudolf Schindler (1887–1953) is often called the "father of gastroscopy", because he carried out much work to explain how the digestive system works. He discovered many diseases based around the human digestive system.

# Reproductive System

## ★ Life Creator

### THE BIG IDEA

The process of combining the sperm of a man with the egg of a woman to produce a new baby.

Hi, I'm Reproductive System, and I'm going to tell you how babies are made. For starters, men and women have different systems that work together.

A man's reproductive system contains millions of sperm, which are produced in his testes. In a woman's body, two ovaries contain hundreds of egg cells. Each month the ovaries release an egg cell. If a man's sperm latches onto the egg cell through sexual reproduction, fertilization may follow. A ball of cells called an **embryo** forms and settles inside the woman's womb. Over time it develops into a **fetus**, and eventually emerges as a baby.

- There are slightly more men than women on Earth; 50.5% of humans are male, and 49.5% are female

- It takes around 39 weeks for a baby to develop inside a woman's body

### SAY WHAT?

**Embryo:** Life in its simplest form as a group of cells, before it starts growing into a baby.

**Fetus:** The name used to describe a baby in the womb, from eight weeks until birth.

### SCIENCE NOW

Different animals produce babies in different ways. While humans give birth to live young, other animals, such as reptiles, lay eggs inside which their babies develop. Some organisms, such as bacteria, simply split in two to multiply!

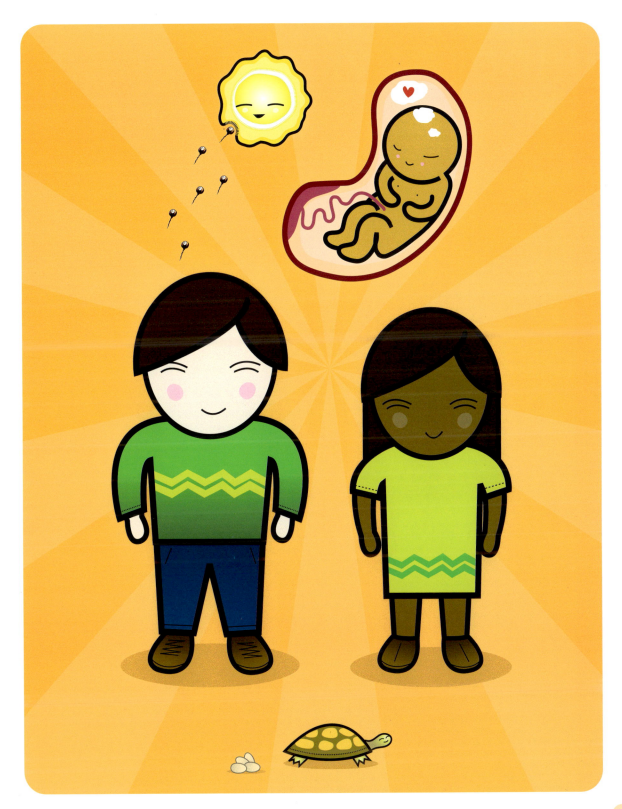

# Urinary System

★ Removals Expert

**THE BIG IDEA**

The process of getting rid of liquid waste from the human body. It passes out of the body as **urine** (wee).

So you want to expel some waste, do you? You'll probably want to use me, Urinary System. I rid your body of harmful waste by flushing it out as fluid. Here's how I do it.

My primary organs are the kidneys, essentially a pair of filters. They remove a waste substance called urea from your blood as it passes through them. The kidneys then transport the waste as urine to your bladder, where it is stored. Once your bladder is full and you feel the need to pee, you go to the toilet and the urine leaves your system.

- An adult gets rid of up to 2 litres (3½ pints) of urine per day

- The average person goes to the toilet 1400–2500 times a year

- Our kidneys process blood at a rate of 1800 litres (3200 pints) a day

**SAY WHAT?**

**Urine:** Excess water, salt and other bodily waste combine to make a watery fluid that is yellow in colour.

**SMART SCIENTIST**

A German pharmacist called Henning Brand discovered the element phosphorus in 1669 using urine. He was trying to turn things into gold, but he found that when he boiled urine, it left behind a substance when it was mixed with oxygen – phosphorus!

**Atom**

**Mass**

**Weight**

**Energy**

**Force**

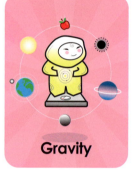

**Gravity**

**Speed**

**Electricity**

**Magnetism**

**Sound**

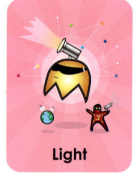

**Light**

# Physics Crew

The universe is the most incredibly amazing place.
Seriously, there are so many fascinating things going on
around you . . . *all the time*. Have you ever wondered
how everything works? Well, you're about to find out.
The members of this clever Physics Crew range from
just-so-tiny-you-can't-see-it Atom, to mystical, magical
Light and Gravity. And if "cool" is your thing, wait until
you meet Magnetism. Human beings have been delving
into the workings of the universe for thousands of years.
And thanks to this talkative bunch of science buffs,
its secrets are about to be revealed to you, too!

# Atom

## ★ Matter Maker

**THE BIG IDEA**

The smallest, most basic form of any **element** in the universe.

Everything in the universe is made of matter – you, your clothes, the trees, the planets – *everything*. But what is matter made of? Well, it's made of me, Atom. And inside me are even smaller bits of matter called particles: these are protons, neutrons and electrons.

What kind of atom I am depends on the number of particles I have – in particular, the number of protons. For example, a carbon atom has six protons, but an oxygen atom has eight. I would ask you to count them, but they are so tiny you could never see them. Ha! I'm thousands of times thinner than human hair!

- ◉ It might be unbelievable, but an atom is 99.9% empty space

- ◉ You have seven billion billion billion atoms in your body

**SAY WHAT?**

**Element:** A substance made of just one kind of atom, such as iron, oxygen or carbon.

**✳ SMART SCIENTIST ✳**

In the 5th century BCE, Greek philosopher Democritus suggested that everything must be made of smaller parts, which he called atoms. He wasn't completely right, though. He thought atoms were indestructible, but we now know that isn't true!

# Mass

## ★ Heavy Lifter

### THE BIG IDEA

A measure of the amount of matter in an object, given in kilograms or pounds.

Hi, I'm Mass. You've met my pal Atom? Well, I measure matter, which means I can tell you how many atoms there are in an object. The more matter something has – whether it's an egg, or a ball, or a planet – the greater its mass.

Unlike my friend Weight on the next page, I don't depend on **gravity**. In other words, my measure is the same no matter where in the universe that egg, ball or planet is. Weight and Gravity will explain this in more detail. The main thing is, I can help work out how much force is needed to get something moving.

- Black holes are the most massive objects in the universe – some are billions of times more massive than our sun!

- Some particles that transport certain forces are known to be massless

### ⚡ SAY WHAT? ⚡

**Gravity:** The force between two objects caused by them both having mass. Anything with mass is attracted to everything else. The more mass something has, the more it attracts.

### ✳ SMART SCIENTIST ✳

We have Isaac Newton to thank for much of our knowledge about the universe. A famous scientist, Newton wrote about the laws of motion in the 17th century. His second law talks about the amount of force needed to move an object.

# Weight
## ★ Gravity Gainer

**THE BIG IDEA**

A measure of the force of gravity on an object.

I have much in common with Mass, but we are not the same. I'm Weight, and I'm what happens when you take Gravity into account. So what does that mean?

Well, on Earth you're constantly pulled down to the ground. That's because Earth is **massive** and so has a lot of gravity. I'm worked out by multiplying one object's mass (say yours) by the gravitational pull of another object (in this case Earth, which happens to be 9.8 m (32 ft) per second squared). Gravity varies across the universe, but because it is the same everywhere on Earth, we talk about weight on our planet, rather than mass!

- ◉ A large African elephant can weigh as much as 80 people

- ◉ Our moon has one-sixth of Earth's gravity. So if you weighed 60 kg (132 lb) on Earth, you'd weigh just 10 kg (22 lb) on the moon

**SAY WHAT?**

**Massive:** In physics, the term massive doesn't necessarily mean "huge". It is used to describe an object with a large mass, so it can mean bulky, heavy or solid.

**SCIENCE NOW**

Mass and weight can tell you how much matter something has. To find out how packed in that matter is, we use "density". It's a measure of how matter is spread out in a space. The more packed together something is, the higher its density.

# Energy
## ★ Hard Worker

**THE BIG IDEA**

The ability of anything in the **universe** to do work, to move or to grow.

Hi, I'm Energy. Anything (and everything) that moves, works or grows uses me. I get just about everywhere and I come in many different guises. Let me explain.

You need energy to get up in the morning and make your way to school. Luckily, food contains energy, and your body makes use of this when you eat it. And think of a piece of wood. Boring, huh? Not at all! It's chock full of energy. Burn it, and it releases energy as heat and light. The coolest thing about me is that I cannot be destroyed or created. Instead, I transfer from one form to another depending on where I'm needed.

- ◉ One of the most energetic things in the whole universe is a type of exploding star

- ◉ The word "energy" comes from the Greek word *energeia*

**SAY WHAT?**

**Universe:** Everything that exists, including all objects and energy, throughout time and space. It stretches back to a huge event known as the big bang, 13.8 billion years ago.

**\* APPLYING SCIENCE \***

There are many different types of energy in the universe. Sound energy creates noise, while heat energy releases heat. Chemical energy is stored in atoms. And light energy is how we are able to see things.

# Force

⭐ Mover and Shaper

## THE BIG IDEA

An action, such as pushing, pulling or lifting, that causes an object to move or change shape.

Push on a door and it opens. Kick a ball and it flies into the air. Squeeze putty and it moulds to the shape of your hand. What do these actions have in common? ME! I'm Force, and I make something move or change shape when you push, kick or squeeze it.

You're about to meet my pal Gravity. Well, that's a force and it's acting on you right now – pulling you downwards. But I come as three other types, too. If I am balanced, things remain **stationary** or move at a steady speed. It's when I am unbalanced that things start to move.

- ◉ The strong nuclear force – the force between atoms – is the strongest

- ◉ The heaviest thing a person has ever lifted was a weight of 2844 kg (6270 lb), the same as 45 people

## ⚡ SAY WHAT? ⚡

**Stationary:** Any object said to be at rest and not moving is stationary. Either it has no forces acting on it, or all the forces are balanced.

## ✳ SCIENCE NOW ✳

There are four forces in the universe: gravity, weak nuclear force, strong nuclear force and electromagnetism. Together these forces explain how everything in the universe moves and changes speed!

# Gravity

★ Great Attractor

**THE BIG IDEA**

One of the four forces of nature, gravity explains how anything with mass is attracted to anything else with mass.

You've met my friend Mass? I'm Gravity, the force between objects with mass. You see, any one object with mass is attracted to all other objects with mass. It's me that pulls you towards Earth – but Weight has already explained that, right? You also pull Earth towards you, but by such a tiny amount that the planet doesn't notice it!

I'm useful for explaining how Earth and all the other planets in our **galaxy** orbit our sun. The sun is much more massive than the planets and so pulls them towards it. But I'm not just holding our galaxy together – I operate across the whole universe!

- ◉ Gravity is the weakest of the four forces of nature

- ◉ Even a fridge magnet is stronger than gravity (if it weren't, the magnet would fall!)

**⚡ SAY WHAT? ⚡**

**Galaxy:** A cluster of millions, sometimes billions, of stars. There are trillions of galaxies in the universe. Our sun belongs to a galaxy called the Milky Way.

**✳ SCIENCE NOW ✳**

Black holes are massive, and they have super-powerful gravitational strength. In fact, the pull of gravity from a black hole is so strong that nothing – not even light – can escape its grip if it gets too close!

# Speed

★ Mega Mover

**THE BIG IDEA**

A measure of how fast something is moving.

Zoom! Did you just see that car whizz past? How fast was it going? Ask me, Speed. I just need to know two things: how far the car has travelled and how long the journey took. Say the car has driven 100 km (60 miles) in one hour. I divide distance by time to arrive at 100 kmh (60 mph).

That's pretty basic, but you can use my trick to work out other things. For example, if you know the speed a car is travelling at and how long it spends on the road, you can work out the distance covered by the end of its journey. A car going at 80 kmh (50 mph) for two hours travels 160 km (100 miles) in total.

- ◉ The fastest land speed achieved on Earth was 1228 kmh (763 mph) by a car called the ThrustSSC in 1997

- ◉ In space, speeds of 343,000 kmh (213,000 mph) have been known

## SAY WHAT?

**Velocity:** The term used to describe the speed of an object travelling in a certain direction.

## * APPLYING SCIENCE *

Speed describes something travelling in a constant motion. If the speed increases, we call that acceleration. A decrease in speed is called deceleration.

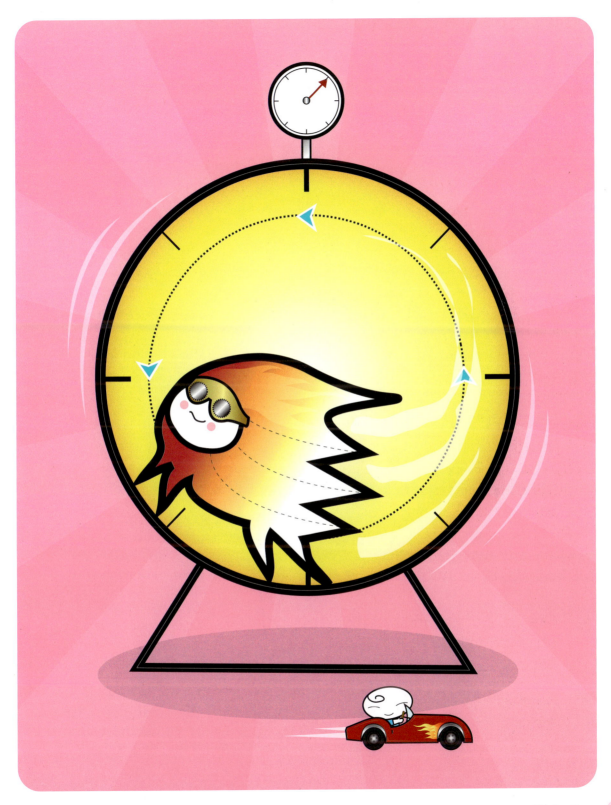

# Electricity

## ★ Super Charger

### THE BIG IDEA

A form of energy carried by **electrons**. It can be used to power devices.

You play video games and watch TV, but do you know how these devices work? It's thanks to the magic of me, Electricity. I'm one of Energy's many guises. At my most basic level, I'm a flow of particles from one place to another – electrons between atoms to be precise. When they move, electrons produce an electric **current**.

Some materials conduct electricity, which means they can carry it. Some, such as copper, are good conductors. Bad conductors, such as wood, are called insulators. Even you conduct electricity, which is why you have to take care when I'm around.

- One bolt of lightning carries enough electricity to make 100,000 slices of toast

- Electricity moves slightly slower than the speed of light (see page 68)

### SAY WHAT?

**Electron:** A tiny particle inside an atom. It has a negative electrical charge, and transmits electricity.

**Current:** The flow of electricity in a circuit.

### ✳ SMART SCIENTISTS ✳

Some say American scientist Benjamin Franklin discovered the principles of electricity in 1752, when he showed that lightning was electricity. But it wasn't until the following century that Italian Alessandro Volta and others discovered how to use electricity.

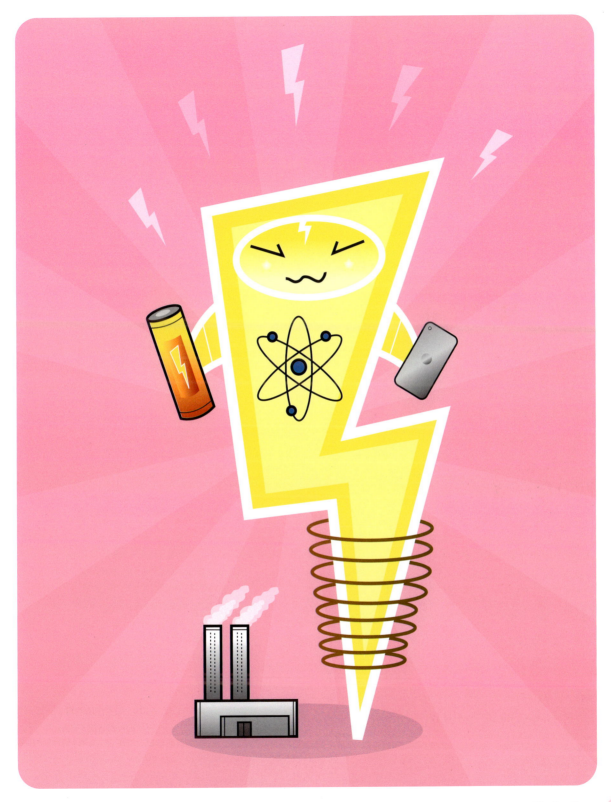

# Magnetism

★ Push-me-pull-me Pal

**THE BIG IDEA**

A flow of current that creates a **magnetic field**.

Hold two magnets close to each other, and they will either pull towards one another or push each other away. This is all down to me, Magnetism.

Here's how I work. A magnet has two ends, called poles: north and south. A magnetic field is the area close to a pole, where my force is felt the strongest. Two of the same poles repel each other, while opposite ones attract. Like my friend Electricity, I'm caused by a flow of electrical charges inside me. Some materials, such as iron, are very magnetic, while others, such as paper, are not magnetic at all.

⦿ The strongest magnetic field in the known universe surrounds a collapsed star, called a neutron star

⦿ Earth's north and south magnetic poles are constantly on the move

**SAY WHAT?**

**Magnetic field:** The area near a magnet within which the force of the magnet can be felt either pulling or pushing.

**SCIENCE NOW**

Planet Earth is magnetic. Inside the planet is an iron core, which produces a magnetic field around it. That's why Earth has a north magnetic pole and a south magnetic pole.

# Sound

## ★ Noisy Neighbour

### THE BIG IDEA

The way in which humans are able to hear music, speech and other noises as they travel through the air.

So, you're watching someone play guitar, and you're thinking, how can I actually hear that? I'm Sound, let me explain.

I am produced when something vibrates really fast, causing particles in the air to vibrate too. The particles vibrate in waves that eventually reach your ear. Your eardrum turns the vibrations into a signal to let your brain know you're hearing something. In the case of the guitar you're listening to, the vibrating strings kick the whole process off. The bigger the vibrations, the louder the sound. The pitch of the sound – whether it is high or low – depends on its **frequency**.

- One of the loudest events in recent history was the Tunguska event in 1908, when a comet exploded above eastern Siberia, in Russia

- The speed of sound is 343 m (1125 ft) per second

### SAY WHAT?

**Frequency:** In the case of vibrations that create an audible wave, this is how often something moves back and forth. The more vibrations, the higher its frequency and the higher the pitch.

### ✳ SMART SCIENTIST ✳

In the 17th century, English scientist Robert Boyle first understood how sound travels. Placing a bell in a jar, he sucked the air out and found the bell made no sound on ringing. That's because there were no particles to vibrate. He realized that air itself carries sound.

# Light
## ★ All-Seer

### THE BIG IDEA

A form of energy that allows humans to see things. It travels at 300,000 km (186,000 miles) per second.

How do you see things? Let me tell you – my name is Light. Like my friend Sound, I'm produced when things vibrate. In my case, a vibrating electric and magnetic field produces a wave of light. I come as many different types, depending on the distance between the peaks of these waves. That is, I depend on their **wavelength**.

I have a number of exotic-sounding forms that include infrared and ultraviolet, but you are probably most familiar with visible light. This is transported on tiny particles called photons. When these photons hit your eye, they allow you to see things.

- It takes about eight minutes for light from the sun to reach Earth

- Things moving away from us in the universe, such as distant galaxies, have their light "shifted" towards the colour red. We call this redshift

### SAY WHAT?

**Wavelength:** The distance between two crests of a wave. The shorter the wavelength something has, the higher its frequency, as there are more waves one after the other.

### SMART SCIENTIST

In 1999, Danish physicist Lene Hau used a cloud of super-cold atoms to slow a beam of light to just 61 kmh (38 mph). Two years later, in 2001, she was able to stop a beam of light completely!

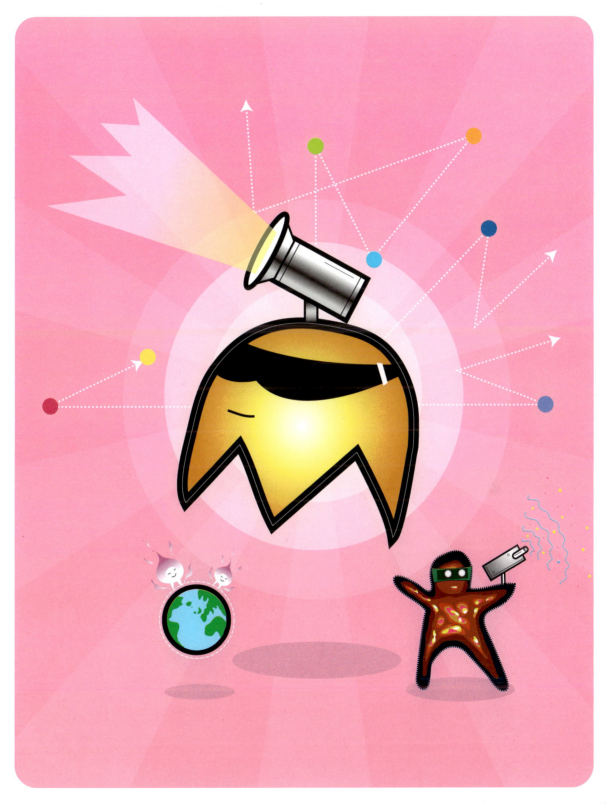

**Element**

**Solid**

**Liquid**

**Gas**

**Chemical Reaction**

**Compound**

**Mixture**

**Melting Point**

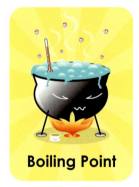

**Boiling Point**

**Catalyst**

**Combustion**

# Lab Rats

It's time to meet the Lab Rats, a zany bunch of characters who inhabit the world of chemistry. Everything kicks off with the smallest of them all, Element, before working up to different states of matter that include Solid, Liquid and Gas! Find out how these types work with one another to make Compound and Mixture. But watch out! Things could get explosive, especially by the time you catch up with the likes of Boiling Point, Chemical Reaction and Combustion. . .

# Element

## ★ Chemistry King

### THE BIG IDEA

A **substance** made of just one kind of atom (see page 48), such as iron, oxygen or carbon.

Hi, I'm Element. You'll find me all over the universe, because everything is made of me. I am the simplest, most basic form of any given substance.

You may remember from Chapter 1 that I am made of atoms. Well, inside each type of me, Atom's particles – the protons, neutrons and electrons – follow a very precise arrangement. That means each element (118 are known about so far) is unique. It also has its own symbol: H for hydrogen and O for oxygen, for example. Sometimes elements combine together to make a new substance – but more on that later!

- ◉ Most elements occur naturally, while others can only be made by scientists in a laboratory

- ◉ Six new elements were formally recognized in 2016

### SAY WHAT?

**Substance:** Any type of matter with its own unique properties. A substance made from a mix of elements is called a compound (see page 82).

### ✳ SMART SCIENTIST ✳

In 1869, Russian chemist Dmitri Mendeleev presented his periodic table to the Russian Chemical Society. It was a chart showing all the elements listed in order of increasing atomic number, which is based on the number of protons in the nucleus.

# Solid

⭐ Chunky Character

**THE BIG IDEA**

Any substance that doesn't flow and remains unchanged when nothing is acting on it.

Physics Crew member Atom can be arranged in many ways to make different substances. When atoms are packed really tight, they make me, Solid.

Left alone, I'm a chunky dependable type that almost always stays as a single object with a fixed shape and takes up the same **volume**. But introduce a force of some kind – say you heat me or cut me in two – and then I can change shape. There are many different types of solid. Some, such as paper, are easy to break or cut. But others, such as diamond, are really tough.

◎ The strongest solid in the world is graphene; a one-atom-thick sheet is at least ten times stronger than steel

◎ The metal gallium is solid at room temperature, but will melt in your hands

**SAY WHAT?**

**Volume:** The amount of space that something occupies. It is measured in three dimensions: height, length, width.

**SCIENCE NOW**

Some substances are able to change state between solid, liquid and gas. These processes have different names. A solid becoming a liquid is called melting. A liquid turning to a gas is evaporation. And a solid turning to gas is called sublimation.

# Liquid

## ⭐ Fluid Fun

### THE BIG IDEA

A flowing substance with a fixed volume that can move from place to place.

You've met my friend Solid, but I'm more of a smooth operator! I'm Liquid, a substance that flows and moves.

I have a fixed volume but no form, which means I can take the shape of anything I'm poured into. Inside me, Atom is packed closely enough that I always stick together. Freeze me, and I turn into Solid – say when water turns to ice. Heat me up and I become Gas (think, steam). I often form into droplets due to something called **surface tension**. And while I might be common on Earth, I'm really rare elsewhere in the universe.

⊙ Humans are made of up to 60% liquid water

⊙ Only two places in the universe are known to have bodies of liquid on their surface – Earth and Saturn's moon Titan

### ⚡ SAY WHAT?

**Surface tension:** The ability of the particles in a liquid to attract one another, sometimes forming droplets.

### ✳ SCIENCE NOW ✳

There's a metal that's one of a kind, and it's called mercury. It is the only metal that's a liquid at room temperature.

# Gas

## ⭐ Free Spirit

**THE BIG IDEA**

A substance whose particles can move freely in the air.

Now you've met Solid and Liquid, I'd like to introduce myself, too. I'm Gas, a substance that can move around in the air.

A real free spirit, I can take any shape that suits me. I can get bigger and smaller, because my **molecules** are moving around all the time, just loosely attracted to one another. Put me inside a container, and I'll spread out to fill it, but release me into the air and, whoosh – my particles race off in different directions. All my forms share the same properties, but while you can see some gases, others are invisible. We just love doing our own thing!

- ◉ The most common gas in Earth's atmosphere is nitrogen, which makes up 78%; oxygen is next at 21%

- ◉ Tungsten hexafluoride is a really heavy gas that sinks like a stone

**SAY WHAT?**

**Molecule:** A group of two or more atoms that have been bonded together. It's normally the smallest amount of something that can form a chemical reaction.

**SCIENCE NOW**

One other state of matter exists, aside from solid, liquid and gas. It's called plasma, and it's a type of hot gas that's full of charged particles. You don't know it, but you see plasma every day – up in the sky. That's right, our sun is a giant ball of the stuff.

# Chemical Reaction

⭐ Energy Exploder

## THE BIG IDEA

When a change of energy between elements produces something new.

When your apple goes rotten and starts to turn brown, that's me, Chemical Reaction. Drop a sugary sweet into a fizzy drink, and you'll find me there, too. Let me tell you more.

All molecules have a certain amount of potential energy in them (potential just means it is waiting to be used). The more energy there is, the more likely it is to do something. I occur when the atoms in a molecule get rearranged and form new chemicals. Sometimes they need help, such as applying heat. The results can be slow, like rusting, or explosive – like a bomb going off. Ka-boom!

- ◉ Russia's Tsar Bomba, a bomb detonated in 1961, is the largest ever man-made explosion; it destroyed buildings 55 km (34 miles) away

- ◉ Food is digested in your stomach thanks to **chemical** reactions

## ✳ APPLYING SCIENCE ✳

Some everyday substances are products of a chemical reaction. For example, table salt is made when two elements, sodium and chloride, react together. And rust is caused by metal reacting with oxygen in the air.

# Compound
## ★ Cool Combiner

**THE BIG IDEA**

The **product** when two or more elements are combined during a chemical reaction.

What happens when two or more elements combine? You get me, Compound! I come about when my friend Chemical Reaction joins the party.

For example, two atoms of hydrogen react with one atom of oxygen to make the molecule $H_2O$ (that's water to you). Many different forms of me exist, and sometimes I can even be split using Chemical Reaction to return me to my original component forms. Large numbers of molecules join together to make Solid, Liquid or Gas. See, we all work together in the end.

**SAY WHAT?**

**Product:** In chemistry, the outcome when two or more reactants combine to produce something new.

**SCIENCE NOW**

Not all elements in the periodic table can react to form compounds. For example, some gases do not bond easily with other things. These include helium, neon and krypton.

- ◉ Some compounds have strange names. For example, "housane" is so called because its structure looks a bit like a house

- ◉ Certain compounds, such as water, need huge amounts of energy to break them apart

# Mixture
## ★ Great Combo

**THE BIG IDEA**

The product when two or more elements are combined without needing a chemical reaction.

Hi, I'm Mixture. I combine two or more elements but, unlike Compound, I have no need for Chemical Reaction.

I come about when substances blend together. For example, stir salt into water, and you'll make lovely Liquid in which all of the salt has **dissolved**. My beauty lies in the fact that I can be reversed quite easily. To remove all that salt you just added, boil me. Liquid turns to Gas leaving the Solid, salt, behind! The best news? I use way less Energy than Compound, giving that Physics Crew hero a well-earned rest.

◉ A river creates a mixture of rock, sand and soil as it travels to the sea, often carving out a path as it goes

◉ Sand itself is a mixture of lots of tiny rocks, all broken down

**SAY WHAT?**

**Dissolve:** When a substance joins with a liquid or gas to become a solution. All solids, liquids and gases can dissolve.

**✳ APPLYING SCIENCE ✳**

Mixtures are not always obvious. Smoke is a mixture of different particles in the air, for example. Foam is gas trapped in a liquid. And even blood is a mixture of plasma (a yellowish liquid) and red blood cells.

# Melting Point
## ★ Super Oozer

**THE BIG IDEA**

The **temperature** at which a solid turns to a liquid.

Phew, is it hot in here? Increase the temperature of something, and it heats up. When you boil an egg in a metal pan, for example, the pan gets hot. But what if it got really, really hot? Well, then the metal would start to melt and turn into a liquid . . . by which time it will have reached me, Melting Point.

When the temperature of a substance increases, Atom gets really excited. Instead of staying stuck together as Solid, atoms start to flow freely as Liquid! Some substances, such as ice, have a very low melting point, whereas in others, such as iron, it is super high.

◉ The metal with the lowest melting point is mercury. It melts at just −39°C (−38.2°F)

◉ When temperatures go higher than melting point, they reach boiling point (see page 88)

**SAY WHAT?**

**Temperature:** A measure of how hot or cold a substance is.

**SCIENCE NOW**

The element with the highest melting point is tungsten, which melts at a whopping 3414°C (6177°F). But in 2015, scientists came up with a new material that would melt at more than 4250°C (7680°F), two-thirds the temperature of the sun's surface. Scorcher!

# Boiling Point
## ★ Bubble Trouble

**THE BIG IDEA**

The point at which a liquid is heated to make it turn into a gas.

If you have ever seen a pot of hot water bubbling away, you've seen me in action. I'm what happens when Liquid is heated to such a high temperature that it turns into Gas. Call me Boiling Point.

Once I am reached, Atom starts to get super excited. Liquid evaporates and rises into the air. This happens because the **bonds** between Liquid's molecules break apart, allowing them to change to Gas. Not all liquids have the same boiling point. Water, for example, boils when it reaches 100°C (212°F). Why does boiling Liquid form bubbles? That's the gassy air in the water starting to escape!

⦿ Water boils at a different temperature the higher up you are. At the top of Everest, it boils at 70°C (158°F)

⦿ Liquid helium boils at a mega chilly −269°C (−452°F)

**SAY WHAT?**

**Bond:** The way in which molecules join together. In covalent bonding, atoms share electrons. In ionic bonding, one atom gives an electron to another atom.

**SMART SCIENTIST**

The celsius temperature scale is named after 18th-century Swedish astronomer Anders Celsius. He developed the scale to explain when water either froze or boiled.

# Catalyst
## ★ Reaction Maker

**THE BIG IDEA**

A substance that speeds up a chemical reaction by lowering the **activation energy** involved.

My friend Chemical Reaction is super cool, but it can also be terribly slooooow or require vast amounts of Energy. I'm Catalyst and, well, I speed things up a little.

Essentially, I make more molecules collide together, so that a reaction takes place in less time. For example, hydrogen and oxygen don't normally react with one another. But light a match in a room filled with those gases and they will react (a bit explosively) to form water. The best thing about me is that I don't get used up in a reaction – I am still there, right to the very end.

- ◉ The opposite of a catalyst is an inhibitor; it reduces the speed of a reaction

- ◉ Catalysts are useful because they reduce the amount of energy you need for a reaction

**SAY WHAT?**

**Activation energy:** The minimum amount of energy needed to perform a chemical reaction. It is often achieved by increasing temperature or pressure.

**＊ SCIENCE NOW ＊**

In biology, one type of catalyst is called an enzyme – a protein molecule found in cells. Enzymes speed up chemical reactions in your body. For example, the enzyme amylase, found in saliva, breaks down starch in food when you chew.

# Combustion
## ⭐ Fuel Burner

**THE BIG IDEA**

The process of burning a **fuel** with oxygen in order to produce energy.

Are you ready to explode? I'm here to help! I'm Combustion, the process by which fuel burns with oxygen to produce energy in the form of heat, light or sound.

In a car, the fuel produces energy as heat, which is then used to power the vehicle. Sadly, some of my processes produce nasty gases. For example, that same car powered by petrol or diesel produces carbon monoxide, which is bad for the environment. Some rockets burn hydrogen with oxygen to produce staggeringly huge amounts of energy – enough to raise the rocket off the ground. We have lift off!

- ◉ Combustion was first understood by French chemist Antoine-Laurent Lavoisier in 1772

- ◉ Chlorine trifluoride is one of the most easily combustible things on Earth. It reacts with everything, even glass

**SAY WHAT?**

**Fuel:** Any substance that can be burned to produce power or energy. Wood and gasoline are both types of fuel.

**SCIENCE NOW**

Some types of combustion, such as burning hydrogen with oxygen, are super fast. There are slow types of combustion too, known as smouldering, such as when a piece of wood glows red-hot.

# Glossary

**Acceleration:** An increase in the velocity of a moving object over a period of time.

**Activation energy:** The minimum amount of energy needed to perform a chemical reaction. It is often achieved by increasing temperature or pressure.

**Backbone:** Also called the spine, a set of connected bones that runs down an animal's back. It supports the rest of the animal's skeleton and its body.

**Biome:** An area that contains particular types of plants and animals.

**Bond:** The way in which molecules join together. In covalent bonding, atoms share electrons. In ionic bonding, one atom gives an electron to another atom.

**Carbon dioxide:** The colourless, sour-tasting gas that is a waste product of respiration.

**Cartilage:** A type of tissue that has a similar function to bone, but is softer and more flexible.

**Cell:** The smallest basic unit of a plant or animal. All living things are made up of cells.

**Chemical:** All matter in the universe is made of chemicals. The term "chemical" simply refers to anything that's made of matter.

**Cold-blooded:** Animals that control their body temperature using the surrounding environment.

**Deceleration:** A decrease in velocity of a moving object over a period of time.

**Density:** How compact something is, and how much space it takes up. The more dense a substance is, the heavier it feels for its size.

**Dissolve:** When a substance joins with a liquid or gas to become a solution. All solids, liquids and gases can dissolve.

**Electron:** A tiny particle found inside an atom. It has a negative electrical charge, and transmits electricity.

**Element:** A substance made of just one kind of atom, such as iron, oxygen or carbon.

**Embryo:** Life in its simplest form as a group of cells, before it starts growing into a baby.

**Enzyme:** Inside the human body, a biological molecule that speeds up a reaction.

**Exoskeleton:** A rigid substance that surrounds the bodies of some invertebrates.

**Extinct:** A species that has died out completely, and has no living members left on Earth.

**Fetus:** The name used to describe a baby in the womb, from eight weeks until birth.

**Frequency:** In the case of vibrations that create an audible wave, this is how often something moves back and forth. The more vibrations, the higher its frequency and the higher the pitch.

**Fuel:** Any substance that can be burned to produce power or energy. Wood and gasoline are both types of fuel.

**Galaxy:** A cluster of millions, sometimes billions, of stars. There are trillions of galaxies in the universe. Our sun belongs to a galaxy called the Milky Way.

**Gravity:** The force between two objects caused by them both having mass. Anything with mass is attracted to everything else. The more mass something has, the more it attracts.

**Infection:** Something that enters an animal, like a bacteria or virus, that can cause it harm.

**Lung:** An organ that expands and contracts to draw air into the body. The lungs extract oxygen from the air and pass it into the circulatory system.

**Magnetic field:** The area near a magnet within which the force of the magnet can be felt either pulling or pushing.

**Marrow:** The soft, sponge-like tissue in the centre of most bones. It's the place where new blood cells are made.

**Massive:** In physics, the term massive doesn't necessarily mean "huge". It is used to describe an object with a large mass, so it can mean bulky, heavy or solid.

**Matter:** Everything we can see in the world around us is made of matter.

**Metamorphosis:** A process by which some animals change from a younger form to their adult self – for example when a caterpillar turns into a butterfly.

**Molecule:** A group of two or more atoms that have been bonded together.

**Muscle:** A bundle of tissue and fibres that can contract or relax on receiving a signal via the nervous system.

**Nerve:** A bundle of fibres (a bit like wires) made of long chains of nerve cells. They carry signals around the body.

**Nutrient:** The name given to any substance that helps an organism grow. Humans get their nutrients from the food they eat.

**Oesophagus:** A tube that connects your throat to your stomach.

**Orbit:** A curved path taken by something travelling around a large body, such as a planet or star.

**Organ:** A group of tissues that performs a certain function inside a living thing; the heart or lungs, for example.

**Organism:** Any type of life, such as a plant or animal. It can be made of a single cell, or lots of different types of cells.

**Oxygen:** The third most common element in the universe. Life depends on oxygen to survive.

**Particle:** A really small part of matter, ranging from subatomic things (such as electrons) to larger things, such as particles of dust.

**Photosynthesis:** The process by which plants turn sunlight into energy.

**Segment:** One part of a whole thing. Something can be separated into segments, and each of them adds together to make the whole.

**Species:** A group of living things that are closely related to each other and share many characteristics.

**Stationary:** Any object said to be at rest and not moving is stationary. Either it has no forces acting on it, or all the forces are balanced.

**Substance:** Any type of matter with its own unique properties. A substance made from a mix of elements is called a compound.

**Surface tension:** The ability of the particles in a liquid to attract one another, sometimes forming droplets.

**Temperature:** A measure of how hot or cold a substance is.

**Tissue:** Another word for various materials that make up a living body.

**Universe:** Everything that exists, including all objects and energy, throughout time and space. It stretches back to a huge event known as the big bang, 13.8 billion years ago.

**Urine:** Excess water, salt and other bodily waste that combine to make a watery fluid that is yellow in colour.

**Velocity:** The term used to describe the speed of an object travelling at speed in a certain direction.

**Volume:** The amount of space that something occupies. It is measured in three dimensions: height, length, width.

**Warm-blooded:** Animals that can regulate their own body temperature without relying on the surrounding environment.

**Wavelength:** The distance between two crests of a wave. The shorter the wavelength something has, the higher its frequency, as there are more waves one after the other.

# Index